THE HOW AND WHY WONDER BOOK OF
OCEANOGRAPHY

Written by ROBERT SCHARFF
Illustrated by ROBERT DOREMUS
Editorial Production: DONALD D. WOLF

Edited under the supervision of
Dr. Paul E. Blackwood, Washington, D. C.

Text and illustrations approved by
Oakes A. White, Brooklyn Children's Museum, Brooklyn, New York

GROSSET & DUNLAP • **Publishers** • **NEW YORK**

Introduction

The vast expanses and the impenetrable depths of the ocean have given it a mystery that has always captured the imagination. What is mysterious about space beyond the eyes' span and distance out of arms' reach? Is it the element of danger, the fascination of the unknown, or the ever-elusive horizon? The enigma of the ocean eludes a simple explanation.

With the rapidly growing science of oceanography, however, the seas are gradually revealing their secrets. Much of the new — as well as the old — knowledge about the ocean is presented in this *How and Why Wonder Book of Oceanography*.

There is a good deal more to be fathomed — more about the directions of ocean currents and their effect on weather; the plant and animal life at different depths; the kinds and amounts of minerals in sea water; the evidence of prehistoric life; the mountains on the ocean floor. An armchair oceanographer can think of hundreds of questions. Fortunately, real oceanographers are asking such questions, too. And because each time one question about the ocean is answered, two new ones pop up, the future is exciting for oceanographers.

The *How and Why Wonder Book of Oceanography* helps readers examine what scientists in this field have already accomplished and what they hope to glean from the sea in the future.

Paul E. Blackwood

Dr. Blackwood is a professional employee in the U. S. Office of Education. This book was edited by him in his private capacity and no official support or endorsement by the Office of Education is intended or should be inferred.

Contents

A space traveler will always see more water than land on earth from whatever direction he approaches our planet, or whenever he observes it during his orbit in outer space.

Oceanography—The Science of the Sea

"Water, water everywhere . . ." That is

Why is the ocean often called the "mysterious sea"?

how our planet looks to the astronauts as they circle it in outer space. And there is good reason for this: almost three-fourths of the earth's surface is covered by water. It is hard to believe that all our cities, farmlands, meadows, forests, deserts, and moun-

tains take up only one quarter of our planet's area, but it is true. For this reason, earth is often referred to by scientists as the *water planet*.

Throughout history, the ocean has greatly influenced the affairs of men. It has served as a barrier, as a battlefield, and as a highway for commerce. It has always been a source of food. In modern times, there is even more need

to investigate the sea as an expanding population threatens to exhaust the resources of the land. President John F. Kennedy once stated to the U.S. Congress, "Knowledge of the ocean is more than a matter of curiosity. Our very survival may hinge on it."

Yet the study of the ocean has always been a neglected science. Until our present era, we took it for granted that nothing much was in it. Our present limited knowledge has only helped us to understand the great potential of the sea. Until late 1969, only about two per cent of the ocean bottom had been mapped. This was due to the difficulties of deep-sea exploration. But sonar, undersea television, and small submarines especially designed for deep-sea work, have changed this. At the present time,

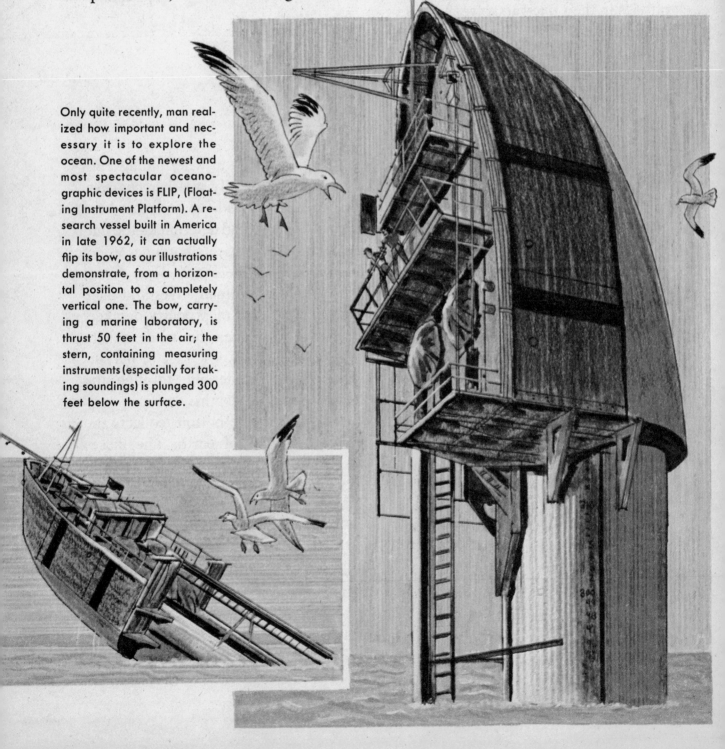

Only quite recently, man realized how important and necessary it is to explore the ocean. One of the newest and most spectacular oceanographic devices is FLIP, (Floating Instrument Platform). A research vessel built in America in late 1962, it can actually flip its bow, as our illustrations demonstrate, from a horizontal position to a completely vertical one. The bow, carrying a marine laboratory, is thrust 50 feet in the air; the stern, containing measuring instruments (especially for taking soundings) is plunged 300 feet below the surface.

the oceans of the world are being mapped and explored at a rapid and ever-increasing rate.

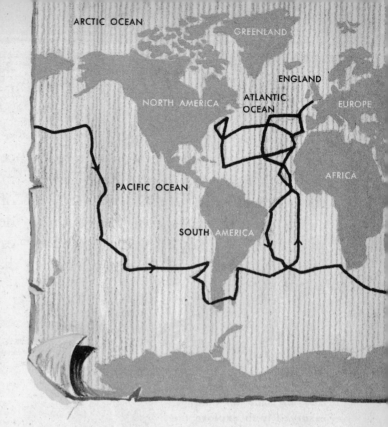

Oceanography is the name given to the study of the ocean.

What is oceanography? Oceanographers — often called the detectives of the sea — use the sciences of biology, geology, chemistry, and physics in their quest to solve mysteries such as where did the ocean come from; what effects does it have on land and the atmosphere; when and from where did sea water come; how many and what species of creatures live in the ocean; is it slowly drying up or getting deeper; and how can man make the most use of it.

The sea is a huge store of raw materials which has barely been tapped. Acre for acre, its animal and plant production could equal that of land, yet man at sea still remains essentially a hunter rather than a farmer. At the present time, only about one per cent of mankind's food comes from the sea. All the known chemical and mineral elements exist in sea water, some in great amounts, yet only salt, magnesium, iodine, bromine, and a few other substances are extracted commercially. Development of a good method of removing the salt so that sea water could be used for irrigation would transform millions of square miles of desert to farming land.

The movement of ocean water serves to regulate the climate on land and plays a large part in determining both long-range and daily weather changes. The ocean's waves have sculptured the edge of the land and determined the outcome of great battles. Shorelines affect the passage of merchant ships. Great waves have taken many lives and have done a great deal of property damage. Below the surface, the modern submariner relies on knowledge of his surroundings to guide him through the dark, unfriendly depths.

Still deeper, the bottom collects the geologic history of earth. The pieces of bone and dust sink to the bottom to form layer upon layer of evidence of a long-past history. Such records on land have been destroyed by the forces of erosion. And in the ocean deeps, where the earth's underlying crust is thinner than beneath the continents, clues to the basic structure of our planet may be found.

To understand and find the answers to all these questions, to develop the

Marine biologist examining samples of ocean water under the microscope.

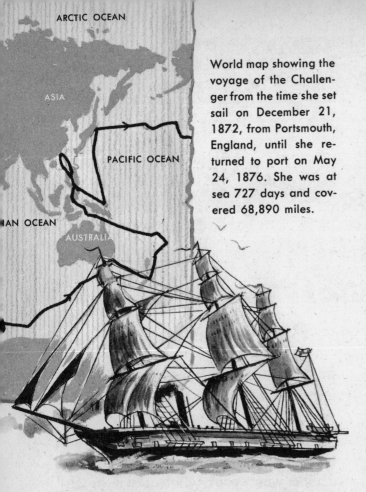

World map showing the voyage of the Challenger from the time she set sail on December 21, 1872, from Portsmouth, England, until she returned to port on May 24, 1876. She was at sea 727 days and covered 68,890 miles.

ARCTIC OCEAN

ASIA

PACIFIC OCEAN

IAN OCEAN

AUSTRALIA

vast resources, or even to consider seriously the possibilities of climate control, it is necessary to study the ocean, the life within it, the air above it, and the bottom below it. The science of oceanography is based on such study.

Interest in the ocean is, of course, by **Who is called the "father of oceanography"?** no means new. Men have been writing and telling sea stories since even before 800 B.C. when the Greek poet Homer described the adventures of Odysseus. But it was an American naval officer, Commander Matthew Fontaine Maury, who in the 1840's and 1850's, first approached the subject scientifically. He charted the currents of the ocean and proved that these immense streams have stability and direction and that they have a great influence on the climate. In short, he taught the sailors of the world how to navigate *with* the seas rather than against them. His book, *The Physical Geography of the Sea and its Meteorology*, published in 1855, was the first ever written on the subject of oceanography, and it is still the basis of our modern science of the sea.

The three and a half year voyage of the **Why was the voyage of the Challenger important to oceanography?** British surveying ship, *H.M.S. Challenger*, was the first deep-sea expedition ever formed to study the ocean, and it set the pattern for most later expeditions. Starting in 1872, the expedition, under the leadership of Sir Charles Wyville Thompson, visited every ocean and collected thousands of specimens of the oceans' floors. The map drawn from these samplings of bottom deposits has not been changed much by the many subsequent explorers. The voyage also established the shapes of the ocean basins. It yielded the first knowledge of currents in all seas, and showed that the temperature of the water was fairly constant in all seasons of the year. The expedition of the *Challenger* demonstrated that the oceans were filled with unknown life waiting to be classified. It proved beyond question that life existed at great depths in the sea. The voyage of the *Challenger* established the methods of research for the great new field of oceanography. Unfortunately, almost 75 years passed before any amount of follow-up work was done on the information obtained from this voyage.

7

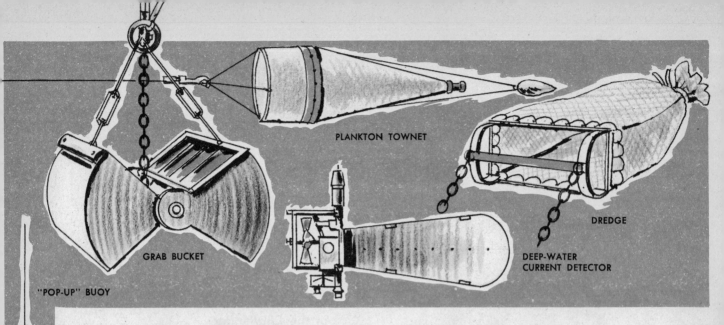

PLANKTON TOWNET

GRAB BUCKET

"POP-UP" BUOY

DREDGE

DEEP-WATER CURRENT DETECTOR

DRIFT BOTTLE

How Oceanographers Study the Sea

Nearly all the American scientists who

How is modern oceanographic research conducted?

concern themselves with marine science are on the staffs of marine and oceanographic laboratories, which is the principal source of employment in oceanography. These seashore laboratories, plus the research ships attached to them, conduct investigations in all aspects of the two major branches of the science: *geophysical oceanography* and *marine biology*.

The geophysical oceanographer studies such things as oceanic circulation, tides, waves, and physical properties of ocean basins and of sea water. The marine biologist, on the other hand, studies the animal and vegetable organisms that live in the sea.

The oceanographer is faced with many special and difficult problems when he goes to sea. The vastness of the ocean itself makes any observational program expensive and time-consuming. It is possible, with specially designed depth cameras, to photograph portions of the ocean's basin. But even a good photograph shows such a very small bit of random data that it does not give a clear picture of the ocean's basin as a whole. It is like trying to decide what your whole town or city looks like by photographing an ant hill in your backyard.

Because of the high cost of ship time and the difficulty of working at sea, the oceanographer puts a premium on simplicity, ruggedness, and the reliability of his instruments. These instruments or tools of the oceanographer can be divided into general classes or groups: those used for making measurements; those employed in collecting study specimens; and those that allow the oceanographer to go below the surface of the ocean for personal observation.

Measuring the depth of water, or taking

What types of instruments are used for making measurements?

soundings, has been done by man ever since the first ships sailed. In the early days, this was done by lowering a heavily weighted line to the sea's bottom. But imagine the difficulty of handling a rope to any great depth. When the crew of the *Challenger* made its famous sounding of 2,435 fathoms in the Pacific, it took them two and a half hours to let out the rope carrying the weight or lead and haul it in again. (A fathom is a nautical measure of depth equal to six feet.) Later, wire cable — which was easier to reel in and out — was used instead of rope. To take a single measure or sounding was still a difficult and time-consuming job. It is not surprising that only a few scientific-minded sailors like Commander Maury and Sir Charles Thompson were willing to take the trouble of measuring and charting the depths of the ocean.

Today, most sounding depends on the timing of an echo. Sonic waves are sent from a ship's transmitter to the ocean bottom; the echo waves return and are picked up by a sensitive receiver. The deeper the water, the longer

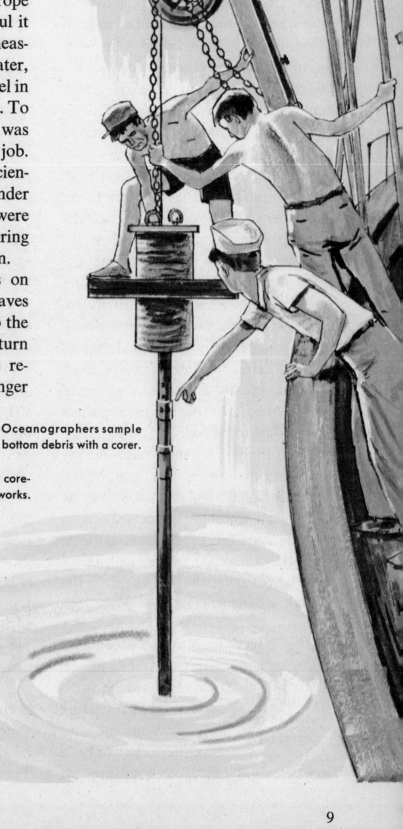

Oceanographers sample bottom debris with a corer.

How the core-sampler works.

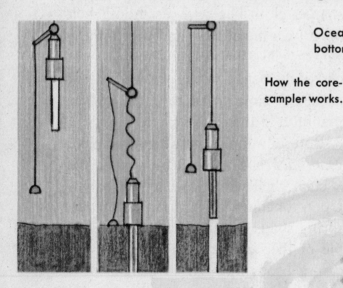

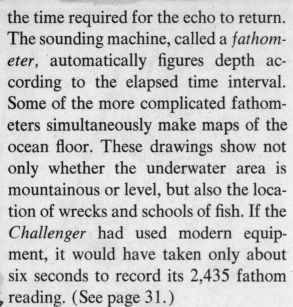

the time required for the echo to return. The sounding machine, called a *fathometer,* automatically figures depth according to the elapsed time interval. Some of the more complicated fathometers simultaneously make maps of the ocean floor. These drawings show not only whether the underwater area is mountainous or level, but also the location of wrecks and schools of fish. If the *Challenger* had used modern equipment, it would have taken only about six seconds to record its 2,435 fathom reading. (See page 31.)

Fathometers indicate the depths of the *apparent* bottom. As we will learn, the *real* or rock bottom is often covered by many feet of sediment. When the oceanographer wishes to measure the depth of the real bottom or the amount of sediment, he must use *seismic soundings.* To do this, two ships are necessary. From one ship, a depth charge of nitro-glycerine or other explosive is set off which creates earthquake waves in the sea bed. A special microphone, called a *hydrophone,* 10 to 25 miles away on the second ship, picks up the echoes of these waves, first from the top of the sediment layer, then from the rock layer's bottom. The second echoes give the measure of the real bottom, while the difference in arrival time of these waves gives the thickness of the layer of sediment. (See page 31.)

The basic tools used by the oceanographer to take samples of oceanic conditions date back many years and have undergone only a very gradual change. Samplings of

What types of instruments are used to take samplings?

plankton (minute plant and animal life), fish, and bottom sediment are still obtained much as they were obtained aboard the *H.M.S. Challenger* in the early 1870's, with *dredges, trawls, nets, grab buckets*, and *coring tubes.*

The *dredge* is a heavy metal frame with a net fastened to it. The lower edge of this frame digs into the sea bottom, loosening plant and animal life that is present there and passing it back into the net behind the frame.

The *trawl* is a large net designed so that its mouth remains open as it is pulled slowly through the water by a ship. It can be made to travel close to the sea bottom so that it can catch some of the more speedy animals that can escape the dredge, or it can be pulled through the water at any other desired depth. Both dredge and trawl are similar to those used by commercial fishermen, although the size of the mesh is sometimes quite small.

The *plankton townet* is a cone-shaped cloth bag with its mouth held open by a metal ring, and with a metal can or glass jar fastened to the small end of the bag. The bag is towed behind a ship at slow speed to catch various plankton in the can or jar container.

Bottom samples are often taken by a *grab-bucket*. This device is shaped like a clam shell with two cup-like halves. Upon touching the bottom, a powerful spring snaps the jaws shut, and a sample of the ocean floor is enclosed and can be brought to the surface.

Still another device for sampling the bottom is a *coring tube*. This is simply a hollow tube that is lowered until it hits the bottom in an upright position. Then, the tube is driven into the bottom by the use of heavy weights or an explosive so that a portion of bottom is forced up into it. When the tube is brought to the surface and opened, the bottom is in its actual form, layer by layer. With the help of such instruments and the samplings they yield, the oceanographer can study the nature of the ocean floor from aboard ship or in his laboratory on shore.

Samples of the ocean water itself can be taken in *Nansen bottles,* named for the Scandinavian explorer-oceanographer, Fridtjof Nansen, who invented them. The cylindrical metal bottle is open at both ends, but has caps or seals that can be closed automatically. When attached to a wire and submerged, water flows freely through the bottle until it has reached the desired depth. A weight is dropped down the wire to trip a device which closes the top and bottom of the bottle, trapping the water within it. When this happens, the bottle turns over and this movement fixes the mercury column in a thermometer fastened to the outside of the bottle. The thermometer thus records the temperature of the water at the instant when the bottle was turned over. In this way, the temperature of the ocean at any depth can be measured. As a rule, a number of such bottles are employed at the same time at various depths. Each bottle, as it closes, releases a second weight which drops to the bottle below, repeating the process.

Formerly, the most common way of **How are ocean currents studied?** tracing direction and speed of ocean currents was by means of *drift bottles.* These were thrown into

the sea containing notes requesting finders to mail them back to those who set them adrift. But bottles now have been replaced by electrical and electronic gear. Buoys containing radio equipment drift in the currents and broadcast signals to two or more ships which plot the paths of the buoys—and, consequently, of the currents — on maps. Or, one or more *flowmeters* are suspended from a cable beneath an anchored buoy. The flowmeters, which are free to turn in the direction of the current, have propellers spun by the moving water. Information on the speed at which the propellers turn and the direction in which the meters face is transmitted electrically to the buoy. All of the information thus obtained is then broadcast to ship or shore stations.

The techniques of underwater photography have been steadily improved and some remarkable pictures of the ocean bottom have been made. Stereoscopic time-lapse cameras loaded with color film are used to obtain almost continuous three-dimensional views of the terrain over which a ship is drifting. Underwater cameras are also used with various bottom-sampling devices or to photograph marine life. In the pitch blackness of the depths, of course, bright lights are needed for photographs except when luminescent creatures are the subject.

The modern oceanographer frequently relies on airborne equipment. Aerial cameras are used to obtain time-lapse movies of the development of clouds, or of changes wrought along a shoreline by storms and other forces. The airborne heat thermometer can measure the surface temperature of the

NANSEN
(REVERSING)
BOTTLES

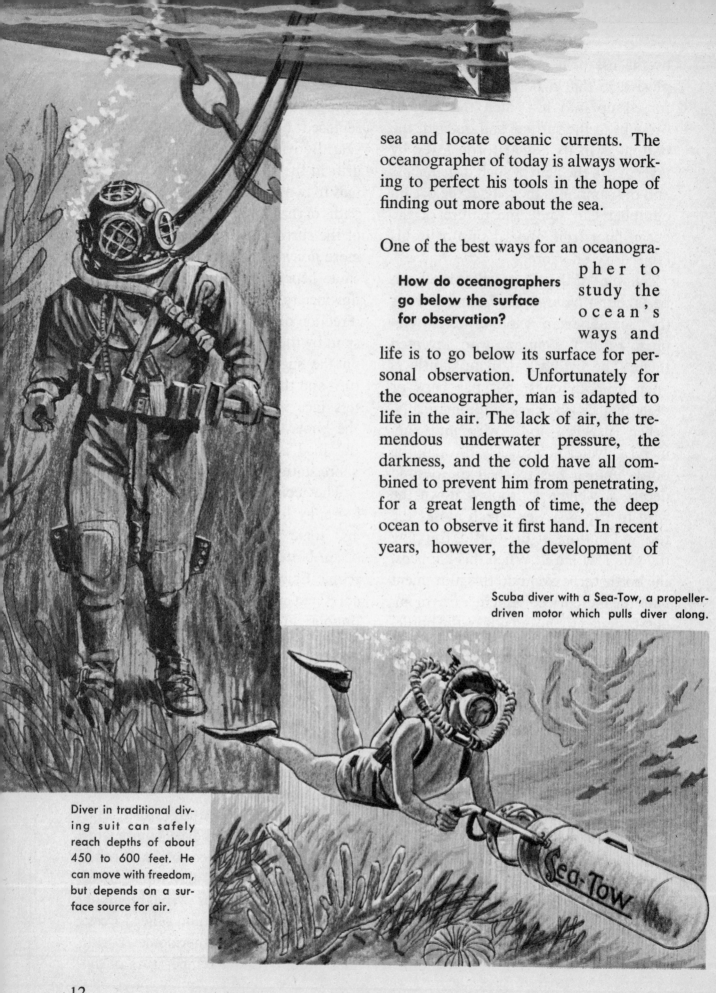

sea and locate oceanic currents. The oceanographer of today is always working to perfect his tools in the hope of finding out more about the sea.

One of the best ways for an oceanogra-

How do oceanographers go below the surface for observation?

pher to study the ocean's ways and life is to go below its surface for personal observation. Unfortunately for the oceanographer, man is adapted to life in the air. The lack of air, the tremendous underwater pressure, the darkness, and the cold have all combined to prevent him from penetrating, for a great length of time, the deep ocean to observe it first hand. In recent years, however, the development of

Scuba diver with a Sea-Tow, a propeller-driven motor which pulls diver along.

Diver in traditional diving suit can safely reach depths of about 450 to 600 feet. He can move with freedom, but depends on a surface source for air.

suitable equipment has to some degree resolved these problems.

There are ways in which the oceanographer can go beneath the surface of the ocean. One is with his diving equipment; the other is in a specially designed underwater craft. Diving equipment, to be suitable for its task, must serve two important functions. It must supply the diver with sufficient air to breathe when underwater, and it must protect him against water pressure while permitting him to move about. To date, no diving apparatus that eliminates these difficulties has been developed.

The traditional diving suit with heavy metal helmet is suitable for depths of about 450 feet. The record descent in this type of suit is approximately 600 feet. While the diver can move about

A battery-driven diving vehicle with a scuba diver astride.

with some freedom, he must depend on a surface source of air. For unlimited freedom of movements, the use of an aqualung or scuba (self-contained underwater breathing apparatus) is best. Instead of depending upon a surface source of air, the scuba diver employs tanks of compressed air which are strapped to his back. Thus, he is no longer dependent on the surface and at once becomes part of the water world. While "free" divers, as scuba divers are sometimes called, have made descents to depths of more than 300 feet, the average range of this apparatus limits the oceanographer to depths of between 200 and 250 feet. Diving with scuba equipment has become a very popular world-wide sport.

In 1970, scientists tried out a device that enabled a diver to breathe the air that is always dissolved in ocean water. If successful, such a device will make it possible for a diver to stay under water without having to worry about how long his supply of oxygen will last, thus increasing the potential for exploration.

To go deeper than the limitations of the two types of diving apparatus will permit, the oceanographer must use an especially designed craft that will protect him from the great pressure found in deep water. The first device of this type, the *bathysphere*, was made in 1930, and used by Dr. William Beebe to study and photograph deep sea life. This first depth ship was a hollow, heavy metal ball made to resist the pressure of the water. It was arranged so that it could be lowered from a "mother ship" on a very long cable, alongside

which was run an electric cable for light and power and a telephone wire by which the men in the bathysphere could communicate with their helpers on board the ship. At the end of the dive, the underwater craft had to be hauled up again by the cable. While dives to depths of 3,028 feet were made in this craft, it was not too successful because practically no freedom of movement for exploration was possible inside it.

The most successful depth ship to date has been the *bathyscaphe*, derived from two Greek words, "bathy" and "skaphe," meaning "deep boat." It was designed by a Swiss professor, Dr. Auguste Piccard, in 1948. The major difference between the bathysphere and

CONNING TOWER
ENTRANCE SHAFT
SNORKLES
BALLAST HOPPERS
PASSENGER SPHERE

the bathyscaphe is that the latter is free to move up and down under its own power, and does not need to be suspended from an enormously heavy cable which could easily break and doom the undersea explorers. The bathyscaphe also has a small electric motor by which it can be moved about over a limited area of the ocean floor. On January 23, 1960, Auguste's son, Jacques Piccard, and naval Lieutenant Don Walsh made man's first descent to the deepest point of any ocean on earth — the Mariana Trench, off Guam Island — within the bathyscaphe *Trieste*. The depth of the dive is recorded as 5,966 fathoms — nearly 35,800 feet.

New types of manned vehicles for exploring the depths have since evolved, and more are being planned. The *Aluminaut,* a 51-foot submersible, creeps along the ocean bottom on wheels, guided by two men inside who also control the craft's long mechanical arms and groping claws which pick up undersea rocks and specimens for study. The Deep-Ocean Work Boat (DOWB), considerably more maneuverable than the *Aluminaut* (yet also holding two men), can hover about in the sea's depths for more than two days. Other depth ships include the 22-foot *Deep Diver,* designed by Edward Link and John Perry, which has a separate pressurized compartment that enables working divers to eat and rest at their convenience and then return to the water outside without an otherwise long period of decompression; *Deep Quest,* combining *Aluminaut's* size and depth capability with *Deep Diver's* "come-and-go" pressurized compartment.

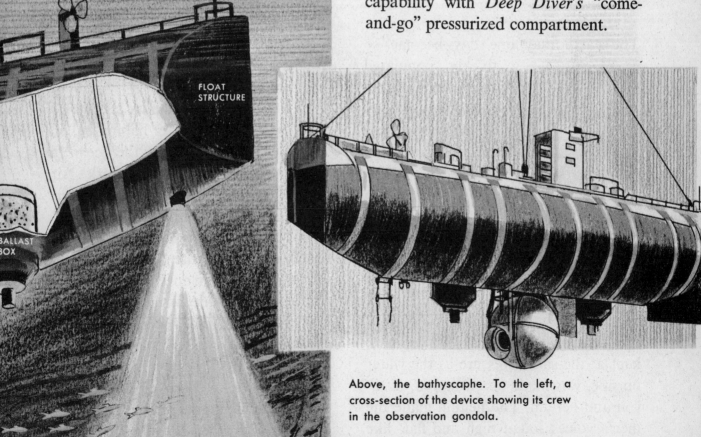

Above, the bathyscaphe. To the left, a cross-section of the device showing its crew in the observation gondola.

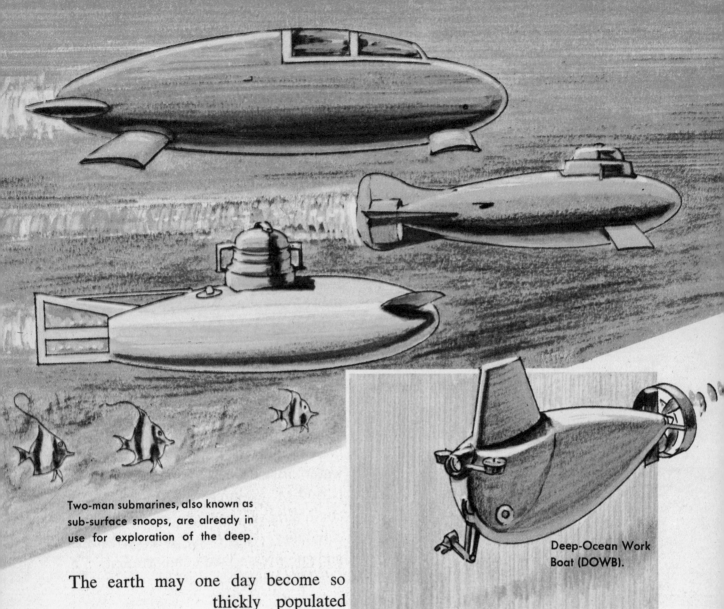

Two-man submarines, also known as sub-surface snoops, are already in use for exploration of the deep.

Deep-Ocean Work Boat (DOWB).

How do men live under water for weeks?

The earth may one day become so thickly populated that men will have to find a way to live in the oceans. Experiments in living underwater are being conducted by men known as aquanauts.

In 1965, off La Jolla, California, three ten-man teams lived 205 feet below the surface in a large tank-like structure named *Sealab II*. Each team lived under water for fifteen days. Two men, one of them being Scott Carpenter, a former astronaut, lived under water for thirty days. The *Sealab's* atmosphere, kept at the same pressure as the water outside, was made up of oxygen, nitrogen and helium. The helium made the men's voices sound high and flat, like the voice of Donald Duck.

In 1969, four aquanauts spent two months in an underwater habitat called *Tektite 1*, 30 feet beneath the ocean in the Virgin Islands National Park. Air pressure in the living and working quarters was kept the same as the water pressure outside. This made it possible for the aquanauts to enter and leave without long waits in an airlock chamber for increasing and decreasing pressures. The aquanauts did not show any ill effects from living so long in pressure higher than that of the atmosphere. In 1970, *Tektite 2*, with 62 aquanauts, 12 of them women, got under way for the purpose of further investigating problems of underwater living.

The World Ocean

What is the world ocean? While there is a great deal that we do not know about the water that covers our earth's surface, we are learning more about it with each passing day. Thanks to the work of oceanographers, and their tools and instruments, we are uncovering answers to questions that have troubled man since the beginning of civilization. Such work is also changing many beliefs about the sea. For example, if you look at a map of the world, you will find that five great oceans are marked off: the Atlantic, Pacific, Indian, Arctic, and Antarctic. While geographers fix these boundaries to the world's water area, oceanographers have recently proven that there is only *one* vast ocean that covers the face of the earth. This they call the *world ocean*. All the so-called "oceans" we see on the maps and globes are really only parts of the world ocean. The continents of the earth — North and South America, Europe, Asia, Africa, Antarctica, and Australia — are thus only islands in this one huge body of water.

How do oceanographers subdivide the world ocean? For easy reference, oceanographers subdivide the world ocean into parts according to the depths of the bottom, distribution of living organisms, currents, climate, and properties such as the amount of salt content of the water.

Using the names given by geographers, most oceanographers refer only to three major subdivisions: the Atlantic, the Pacific, and the Antarctic. Some consider the Indian Ocean separate; others include it as a part of the Pacific and Antarctic Oceans. The Arctic Ocean, all agree, is really a part of the Atlantic. But, remember that all these "oceans" are only parts of the world ocean.

The Atlantic Ocean, believed to be named in honor of the Greek god Atlas, lies like a broad S between North America and Europe, and South America and Africa. It is over 36 million square miles (including the Arctic Ocean), and at its widest point, between La Plata River in South America and Africa, is about 3,700 nautical miles. (A nautical mile is 6,076 feet, while a land mile is 5,280 feet; or a nautical mile is approximately 1 1/7 land miles.)

The Pacific Ocean, a little less than twice the size of the Atlantic, covers more of the globe than do all the continents of the world combined. It is over 9,400 nautical miles in width between Panama and the Philippines and has spots that are over 35,000 feet deep. This ocean was named Pacific, meaning peaceful, by the Portuguese explorer, Ferdinand Magellan. In 1519, Magellan led the first expedition that sailed around the world. He called the waters "Pacific" because they seemed so smooth compared to the rough Atlantic which he had just crossed.

The Antarctic Ocean, often called

the Great Southern Ocean, lies around Antarctica, which includes the South Pole. It is about one-seventh the size of the Atlantic.

The Indian Ocean lies south of Asia and between Australia and Africa. It is almost round in shape, and is about 7/9 the size of the Atlantic Ocean.

Some parts of the world ocean are cut by points of land or by islands and are called seas. The largest sea on the planet earth is the Mediterranean, but even including its several arms (the Aegean, Adriatic, Tyrrhenian, and Black Seas), it is less than one-fifth the size of the Antarctic Ocean. Other famous seas are the Caribbean Sea, which holds the West Indies, and the Bering Sea, which divides Alaska from Russian territory.

What are seas, gulfs, and bays?

Other portions of the world ocean are partly enclosed by land and are called gulfs like the Gulf of California, the Gulf of Mexico, and the Persian Gulf. Bays and sounds are smaller enclosed portions of oceanic waters and include, in the United States, the Chesapeake Bay, Long Island Sound, and Puget Sound. But, seas, gulfs, bays, sounds, inlets, straits, and ocean parts are segments of the one great world ocean just as villages, towns, cities, counties and states are parts of one land.

What is the origin of the ocean?

Many theories about the origin of the ocean have been proposed by scientists. The most widely accepted one is that the earth at some time in its very early history became hot enough to melt the materials from which it was formed. While in this molten state, lighter rock-forming materials floated on the surface of the heavier ones. Then, between four and a half and four billion years ago, the molten earth cooled sufficiently to form a crust of rock that was many miles thick.

Surrounding the earth was an unbroken canopy of clouds miles thick and made up mostly of water vapor. Rain falling toward the still-hot earth was heated to steam and rose to the clouds again. After many millions of years, as the earth continued to cool, its surface temperature fell below the boiling point of water. Rain water could now remain on the earth, covering its whole surface except for the higher places on earth that had been formed from the lighter rock materials.

In 1970, scientists had pieced together evidence that the lighter rock materials had formed one huge continent surrounded by a vast ocean. Then, about 200 million years ago, the great continent began to break up, the pieces moving slowly apart.

The onrushing waters of the single huge ocean now entered and filled the spaces between the separating continents — and became the several oceans and seas we know today.

Why is the ocean salty?

When water comes in contact with soil, it dissolves some minerals. You can prove this by taking a clean saucer and filling it with tap water. Let the saucer stand in a warm place a few days until all the water has evaporated. The film you see on the bottom of the saucer is made by the small amount of mineral matter that is ordinarily dissolved in tap water.

The early world ocean must have been only faintly salty. But, for countless centuries, rain and melted snow have been running over the land, dissolving various minerals, and carrying them down to the ocean. During all this time, the water has been passing through the successive stages of evaporation and condensation that make up the water cycle. (See page 43.) Pure water evaporates from the surface of the ocean and eventually returns to it, carrying various dissolved materials. Thus, the mineral content of ocean water has been increasing ever since the first rainfall.

When we say that the ocean is salty, we mean that its content of dissolved minerals is high. Sodium chloride (common table salt) makes up approximately three-quarters of the dissolved material in ocean water. The remainder is made up of varying quantities of chemical compounds, containing almost every known element. Some of these elements, mainly magnesium and bromine, are now taken from the ocean water commercially. A great deal of the magnesium used in the manufacture of lightweight alloys for airplanes and satellites, for example, comes from the sea. The amounts of the many other minerals in ocean water are so small that it is not yet commercially profitable to claim them. Scientists may yet find ways to make it worthwhile.

The total dissolved salts or *salinity* of sea water varies a great deal in different parts of the ocean. On an average, however, there are 35 parts of salt in every 1,000 parts of sea water or 3.5 per cent.

But, nowhere does the ocean approach the salinity of the Great Salt Lake in Utah (average salt content is about 28 per cent). This landlocked lake is believed to be the last remains of an ancient sea that once covered much of western North America. But, the world ocean in itself, at present, contains enough salts to cover the continents of earth with a layer 500 feet thick.

The upper layers of ocean water may

What are the temperature and color of ocean water?

vary from 29 degrees F. in the polar regions to a high of about 85 degrees F. in the Persian Gulf. (The salinity of sea water lowers the freezing point — which for fresh water is 32 degrees F. — to about 28 degrees F. for sea water.) Along the deep ocean bottom, the water stays at a uniform temperature of about 33 degrees to 34 degrees F. The average temperature of all the water in the world ocean is about 39 degrees F.

In shallow places, the ocean's water appears to be light green or muddy colored, while in deeper sections it seems to be blue, gray, or dark green. These colors change frequently, depending upon whether it is a sunny or cloudy day at the time. Oceanographers know that the water itself has no color; color in the ocean bodies is due only to the reflection of the sky or materials in the water. Some ocean bodies have been given unusual names because they are colored by plant and animal life living in their depths or because muddy rivers flow into them. The Red Sea, the Black Sea, and the Yellow Sea are examples of such names.

Ocean Currents

What are currents? The waters of the world ocean are restless. They are constantly on the move. Sometimes this movement is only up and down, while, in other places, it moves like the waters of a giant river. *Currents,* this general movement of ocean waters, have always puzzled sailing men. As you will remember, it was the currents of the ocean that first interested Commander Maury, and, through his research on them, the whole science of oceanography was started.

The oceanographer of today is still very much interested in currents, although a great deal has been learned since Commander Maury's time. There are two basic types of currents that modern oceanographers are concerned with: the oceanic currents and the tidal currents. Tidal currents, as their name implies, are water movements caused by the rise and fall of the tide.

The rhythmic rise and fall of the ocean's water is referred to as the tide. The tidal range in open water is about three feet, but as it nears land, it may vary from only a few inches to as much as sixty feet.

What causes tides? Along most coasts of the world, twice every day, the waters of the ocean move far up sloping beaches, cover mud flats and marshes, and lift the water level of harbors, inlets, and bays. Twice, the water level gradually goes down,

HIGH TIDE

LOW TIDE

The position of the moon and sun in relation to the earth has a great effect on the tidal range. When sun and moon are at right angles, their gravitational pull tends to cancel each other out, producing a very small tidal range called neap tide. When sun and moon are in line, especially large tides, the spring tides, are caused by the combined gravitational pull.

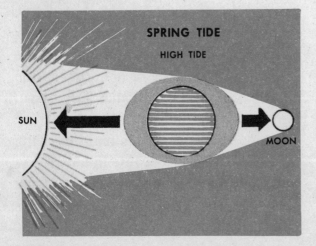

SPRING TIDE

HIGH TIDE

SUN

MOON

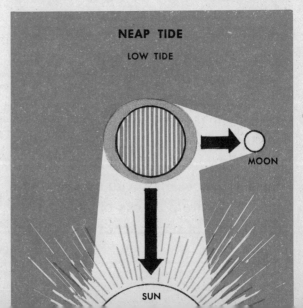

NEAP TIDE

LOW TIDE

MOON

SUN

exposing long stretches of mud, wet sand, and rock. This rhythmic rise and fall of the ocean's water is called the *tide*. The rising or incoming tide at its crest is known as a *high tide,* and the receding or outgoing tide becomes *low tide* when it has reached its maximum retreat. The incoming water is called the *flood* and the outgoing, the *ebb*.

While there are still many questions that remain unanswered about tides, oceanographers tell us their cause is the gravitational force, or "pull," of the moon and sun. While the earth's gravitational force attracts its own waters with a power millions of times greater than that of the moon and sun, their pull, acting on the ocean like enormous magnets, is able to draw the ocean waters into a bulge on the side of the earth to which each is closest. This water, piled up on opposite sides of the earth by the pull of the moon and sun, is known as the *tidal pile* or *bulge*. The height of this pile is called the *tidal range* and is equivalent to about the rise of water at high tide.

Because the moon is closer to the earth than the sun, it exerts the greater influence on the tidal bulge. As a matter of fact, the high tide follows directly beneath the revolving moon. But, to balance this bulge of water on the side of the earth nearest the moon, there is another high tide on the side directly opposite it. Thus, the two great tidal bulges pass continually round the earth in a majestic procession. Conversely, the low tides occur in the regions situated at right angles to these piled-up water masses.

The position of the moon and sun in relation to the earth has a great effect on the tidal range. For example, when the moon and the sun are in direct line with the earth, together they exert their greatest force and thus cause abnormally high tidal range. These tides, called *spring tides,* occur twice each month at the full and new moons. When the moon is closest to the earth, we have exceptionally high tides, called *perigee tides.* When the moon, earth and sun are at right angles to each other, the gravitational pull is weak and the tidal range is small. Thus, these tides, called *neap tides,* are abnormally low. When the moon is farthest from the earth, the tidal range is again very slight and we have exceptionally low tides, called *apogee tides*. (See illustrations on page 20 and immediately below.)

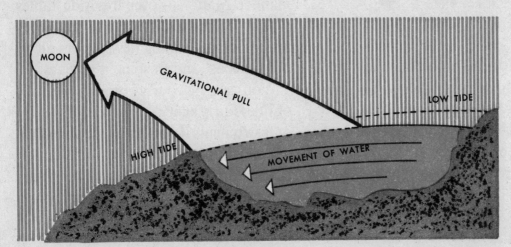

When one shore of an ocean has high tide, its other shore has low tide.

The tidal range varies in different parts of the world. In the

Is the tidal range the same in all parts of the world?

broad expanses of open water, the height of the pile is normally about three feet. But as it nears land, it may vary from only a few inches to as much as sixty feet. The amount of tidal range is a local matter. The moon and the sun set the water in motion, but how high the water will rise depends on local conditions. The tidal range is affected by such things as the slope of the bottom, the width of the entrance to a bay, or the depth of a channel. For example, the tidal range in the Gulf of Mexico is normally only a few inches, but in the Bay of Fundy, an inlet of the Atlantic Ocean extending between New Brunswick and Nova Scotia, the high tide raises the water as much as sixty feet.

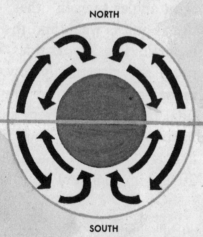

The sun's rays warm the waters of the oceans unevenly. This causes the heated waters of the tropics to move toward the poles in the upper layers of the ocean and polar waters to move toward the tropics along the bottom of the sea.

The reason for this is the difference between the shape and size of the two bodies of water. The Gulf of Mexico is very large, with a gently sloping bottom. The Bay of Fundy has a very narrow channel between high steep walls. When incoming tide flows in the Gulf, it can spread out widely over a large area and thus does not have a chance to pile up very high at any one spot. But, in the Bay, the incoming water does not have room to spread out, and builds up very rapidly to great heights in the narrow channel.

The rhythms of the tide also vary. Oceanographers do not know why a few spots in the world have but one high tide in approximately every twenty-four hours, while the vast majority of the coastlines have two. But, they can predict exactly what time the different tides will occur, thanks to the use of special oceanography instruments which tell

The spin of the earth has certain effects on all moving objects. It causes them to turn slightly to the right in the Northern Hemisphere and to the left in the Southern. Wind and water are affected similarly.

the exact pull of the moon and sun any place in the world. In the United States, the Coast and Geodetic Survey — a governmental agency founded by Commander Maury — prepares tide tables a year or more in advance and they appear in the leading newspapers along our seacoast and in some almanacs.

You can, of course, predict the time of tides fairly accurately without the use of instruments if you know the time they appeared the day before. The moon takes approximately twenty-four hours and fifty minutes to circle the earth, and the high tide will be about fifty minutes later than on the previous day.

Why are tides important?

Tides are important in seaports because large ships must often wait for high tide before they can either enter or leave the harbor. For example,

The combination of three forces, the sun's heat, the spin of the earth, and the winds makes the sea currents circulate clockwise in the Northern Hemisphere and to move counter-clockwise in the Southern Hemisphere.

SOUTH

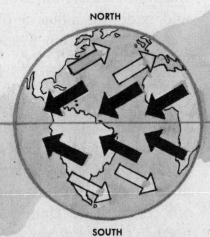

NORTH

Also affected by the spin of the earth and the heat of the sun, the trade winds drive the tropic seas from the east. The Westerlies drive the seas in the higher latitudes from the west.

SOUTH

in the largest port in the world — New York City — all big ships dock or set sail on the high tide.

Tides can have a great effect on salt-water fishing, too. On a high tide, the fish usually swim inshore into the bays to find an abundance of food on bottoms and banks they are unable to reach when waters are low.

Beach areas, which may be entirely out of water at low tide, frequently provide the best feeding grounds at high tide, when the surf or high tide churns up the bottom and uncovers mussels, clams, and other marine food. Weak-fish, striped bass, corbina, flounder, bluefish, and others follow the channels and come within reach of the shore and bridge anglers.

Often, the fisherman will net his best catch approximately an hour before full tide to an hour after. When the tide is on the ebb, the fish retreat to deeper water at the outer edges of sandbars, or to channels that furrow the bays and inlets.

What are the rivers of the ocean?

While tidal currents are the daily forward and backward motion of the sea waters caused by the rhythmic rise and fall of the tides, *oceanic currents* are the constant flow of water in the same direction. These currents are really the rivers in the ocean that flow along on courses that have remained much the same for thousands of years. While oceanic currents have no rocky banks or sandy shores to guide them as do our land rivers, they flow for thousands of miles through areas of comparatively motionless water. Some oceanic currents are so large and powerful that our biggest land rivers, such as the Mississippi, the Amazon, and the Nile, seem like little streams in comparison.

What causes oceanic currents?

Unlike the rivers on land, no oceanic current has a definite source. Heat and cold, sun and wind, and even the rotation of the earth all play a part in forming and keeping these rivers of the ocean flowing. Since the sun does not heat the earth evenly, the ocean water in the tropics is quite warm, while the water at the poles is quite cold. Warm water has the normal tendency to expand and become lighter, while cold water will tend to become more dense and heavier. When the cold water of the poles starts to sink, the warmer water of the tropics flows out away from the equator to replace it. Thus, the heated waters move toward the pole in the upper layers of the ocean, and the polar water goes toward the tropics along the bottom of the sea. But, this natural movement of water would be very slow if it were not for the help of the winds.

If you were to look at a wind map of the world, you would find a series of winds blowing on either side of the equator, always at about the same velocity or speed, and always toward the west. Weather men call them *prevailing winds,* and claim they are caused by the fact that the earth revolves in an eastern direction. These winds push the warm, light water near the equator in a general westerly direction. If there were no land areas on the face of the earth, these wind-blown currents would move steadily westward around the earth on either side of the equator. But, there are continents and islands on earth, and

they act as solid walls that deflect these currents from their course.

In the Atlantic Ocean, for example, the *North Equatorial Current* gathers the warm water north of the equator and, under the influence of the prevailing winds, is driven westward. As the moving water strikes the West Indies, it is divided. While part of it enters the Caribbean Sea, another part turns northward, displacing the heavier and colder polar waters. This latter portion of the current is called the *Gulf Stream* and it moves past Florida and the eastern coast of the United States as far north as Cape Hatteras, off North Carolina. There it veers to the northeast to a point just south of Greenland, where it splits into three major branches. One branch flows northward between Iceland and Greenland into the Arctic. The second moves up between Iceland and Scotland and then past the Norwegian coast into the Arctic. The third branch bends back to the south along the coast of Europe and the upper coast of Africa, joining the *Canary Current*

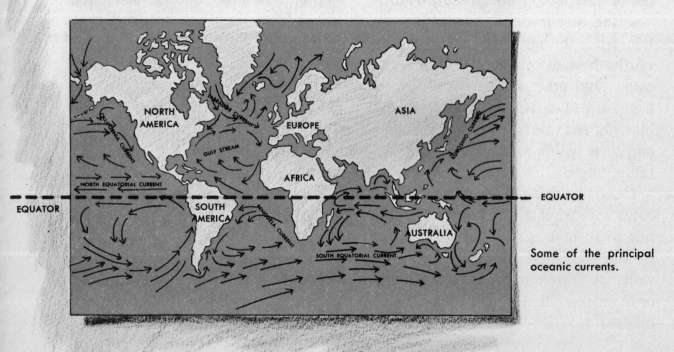

Some of the principal oceanic currents.

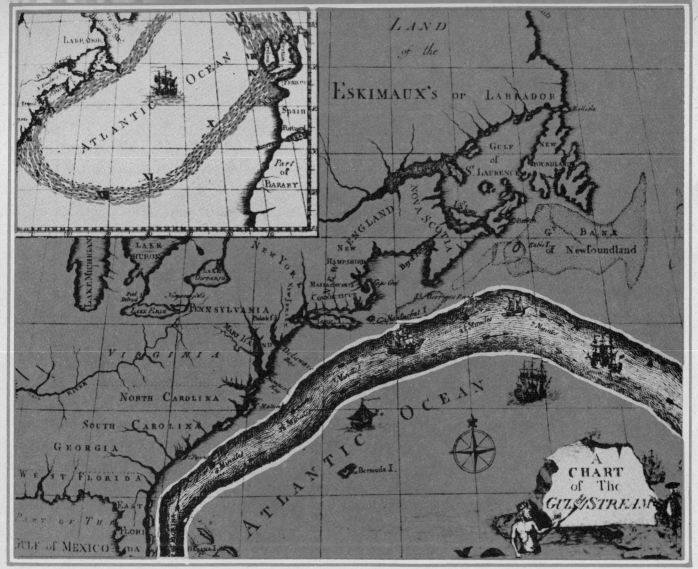

Benjamin Franklin studied the movement of the Gulf Stream. The chart he made of its course, temperature, speed, and depth saved westbound mariners about two weeks in sailing time.

to complete its circular path back to near the equator.

There are major warm and cold water currents in all parts of the world ocean. In addition to the warm water currents in the North Atlantic consisting of the North Equatorial Current, the Gulf Stream, and the Canary Current, the major cold water one is the *Labrador Current*. This current, forming in the Arctic, flows southeastward between Newfoundland and Greenland. It continues in this direction, blown by north-

Where are the principal oceanic currents?

erly winds, along eastern Canada and New England, and it forces the warm Gulf Stream to change its direction off North Carolina. However, because of its heavier, cold waters, the Labrador Current sinks below the Gulf Stream and continues its flow near the bottom until it reaches the region of the equator. Here, the water becomes warm and the current action stops.

The system of currents in the South Atlantic is similar to those of the North Atlantic, except that the open sea in the south makes the southern current, which corresponds to the Gulf Stream, much less regular in its path. The

25

warm waters of the *South Equatorial Current* move across the South Atlantic near the equator to the headland of Brazil where the current divides into two. One part goes north to join the North Equatorial Current, while the southern half, called the *Brazil Current,* follows the eastern coast of South America down toward the South Pole. There, it joins the *Antarctic Current* and returns up the west coast of Africa as the cooling *Benguela Current.*

The currents in the Pacific Ocean are less definitely marked than those in the Atlantic because the Pacific is so large. The North Equatorial Current of the Pacific receives its drive from the prevailing westward winds and continues across the open waters until it strikes the Philippine Islands. There, it swings upward along the Asiatic coast past Japan toward the Arctic. This warm current, called the *Japanese* or *Kuroshio Current,* splits into two branches — one going on toward the Arctic and the other moving eastward across the Pacific toward British Columbia. There, it joins the cold water *California Current* and moves down the west coast of the United States to the equator. This

completes the circular path of the major Pacific Oceanic current.

In the southern hemisphere of the Pacific, there is a similar oceanic current path but the exact path is less clearly defined so it has not been charted accurately as have those of the Atlantic and the northern Pacific. This is true, also, of the Indian Ocean.

Along the seacoasts of the world, **Why are oceanic currents important?** oceanic currents have a great effect on the climate. If you were to look at a map of the world, you would observe that the British Isles are just as close to the North Pole as is a part of Labrador. But the British climate is kept moderately warm by the Gulf Stream, while the inhabitants of Labrador live under a subarctic condition.

California partly owes its famous climate to the cold California Current. Without it, the coast of California might be as hot and dry as the northern part of the Sahara Desert; they are both about the same distance from the Equator. On the other hand, the cold Labrador Current coming down from the Arctic makes the winters of New England and eastern Canada much colder than they otherwise would be.

Ocean Waves

Ever since man first went to sea in **What causes ocean waves?** ships, the rolling waves have both fascinated and puzzled him. They are all over the world ocean. Sometimes they are smooth and gentle,

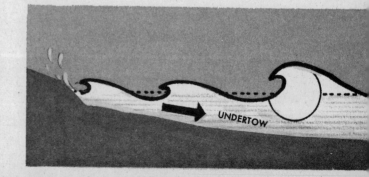

UNDERTOW

at other times high and rough. They have a thousand moods and tricks. It is the hope of oceanographers to eventually be able to predict and thus cope with their various behaviors.

Oceanographers, in their search to find the answers to their many questions, found that most waves at sea are caused by the wind. When the wind blows across the surface of the ocean, it pushes the water into "walls" or "rows" followed by hollows or depressions. The peaks of the wave rows are called the *crests*, and the hollows are called *troughs*. The distance between the crest and trough determines height of the wave.

Waves caused by a storm are referred to as a *sea*. As they travel away from the storm center, they slowly decrease in height, and extend the distances between their crests to many hundreds of feet as they roll shoreward. These long waves are called *swells* and they have a wave action, or rise and fall of the water, that is almost a circular motion. This motion does not, however, extend very far beneath the surface of the water. For instance, during a heavy sea or swells, a submarine submerged underwater will generally experience no water motion at all.

As the waves approach the shore line or shallow water, they are slowed down by the solid earth or rocks beneath, which drags at them like a brake. This causes the swells, or *breakers* as they are now called, to slow down beneath the water while, on the surface, they move along at their former speed. As a result, the breaker movement of the water becomes elliptical, and the distance between the crest and trough increases. The breaker continues to build in height until it breaks up into a roaring mass of foam called a *surf*.

The size of the waves depends on how **How big are waves?** strong a wind is blowing, on how long it blows, and on a third factor called *fetch*. The fetch is the distance in which the wind has blown without hindrance by land.

A strong wind, blowing for many hours, may build up a considerable sea. Add to it a fetch of thousands of miles, and you will have some really big waves. An old sailor's rule of thumb says that the height of the wave in feet will usually be no more than half the wind's speed in miles per hour. For example, in a 60-mile-an-hour gale, the waves would be approximately 30 feet high. Generally, however, waves in the Atlantic seldom reach more than 40 feet, while those of the Pacific rarely rise more than 50 feet. Individual waves, of course, may be far higher. In a Pacific Ocean typhoon, single waves of more than 100 feet are sometimes reported. Such "mountainous" waves are prob-

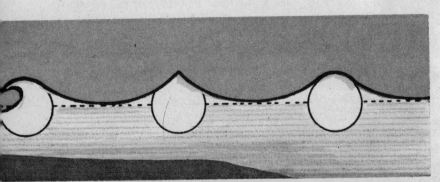

Winds pushing the water forward give the wave its rolling motion. When the wave enters shallow water, it breaks because the drag of the bottom shortens the wave length to twice the depth of the water. Thus, the wave is forced into a peak which breaks when its height reaches more than three times the water depth.

ably caused by several wave peaks sudden piling up, building for an instant one huge mass of water. Waves can rise to a height of only one-seventh of their length before spilling over into white caps. The length of a wave is the distance from one crest to the next.

Wave action may continue in the water long after the wind that has caused it has died down. The reason for this is that waves always move much more slowly than does the wind which caused them.

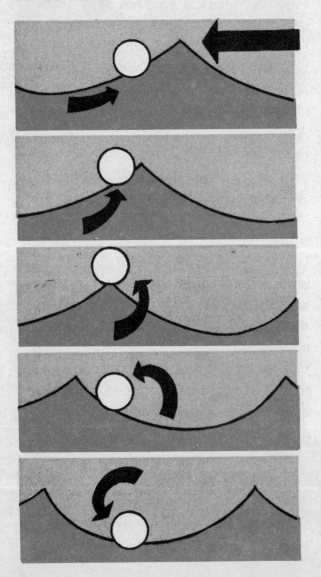

While the water appears to be moving, it actually does not. The water remains in the same spot, but the wave moves through it. To prove it, place a small piece of cork or wood on the surface of a lake a short distance from where you plan to drop a stone. As the ripples reach the cork or wood, it bobs up and down but does not move on with the wave. This shows that the waves are passing through the water, but they are not taking the water with them. Part of the water will move as the waves disturb it, but after the waves have passed, it returns to its original location.

Does water move with the waves?

The fact that waves pass through the

Watch a piece of wood or ball ride out the waves the next time you go to the beach. The position of the ball above shows how the wave travels and that the water does not move. The water motion goes from left to right, the ball moves slightly up the front slope of the wave approaching it, and then slides down the back of it. When the wave has passed, the ball will not have changed its position at all, except perhaps for a couple of inches.

builds up and tears down the land along a coast. Waves make sea caves or sea cliffs, and cut out islands from the shore. They can also be beneficial in many ways, such as moving the sand in the ocean to build sand bars and adding land to shore lines.

While most waves are caused by winds, **What is a tidal wave?** a few are caused by volcanic eruptions and underwater earthquakes. When earthquakes originate beneath the ocean, and abruptly shock the waters of the ocean into action, *tidal waves* may form. These have no connection with the tide, and so they are not "tidal waves" at all. Instead, they are of seismic origin and in recent years have come to be called by their Japanese name, *tsunami*.

Tsunami, the most destructive of all ocean waves, may travel great distances before doing their damage. For example, the tsunami that struck Hawaii a few years ago taking many lives were the results of underwater earthquakes more than 2,000 miles away.

water without taking it with them can be demonstrated by using a fairly heavy piece of rope about 15 feet in length. Fasten one end of the rope to a post. Now, move the free end up and down. The rope will form into waves and seem to travel toward the post. But you know that the rope itself is not moving away from you, since one end is fastened and you are holding the other. Each part of the rope is moving merely up and down. It is the energy of the motion or wave that is moving through the rope from the end in your hand to the end fixed to the post. In the ocean, a drifting boat moves because it is pushed by the wind or is carried by the tidal currents, but never by the wave action of the water.

Waves breaking on the shore have enormous power and a **What effect do waves have on the shoreline?** raging surf can be one of the most destructive forces in the world. It can break up the strongest pier, or pick up a house and carry it out to sea. It is the power of the surf that

Tidal bores are caused by the blocking of rising tides on the **What are tidal bores?** seaward side at a river's mouth by sand bars. As the water gathers offshore from the sand bars, it builds up pressure which finally allows it to spill over the sand bar, sending a large wave or wall of water rushing up the river. Most tidal bores are harmless but the bore of the Tsientang River in China is often dangerous, with waves that sometimes rise as high as 25 feet.

The Ocean's Basin

At one time, it was believed that the ocean's bottom was a huge, scooped-out hole which was nearly smooth. Now, thanks to the recent work of oceanographers, we know the bottom of the world ocean is divided into three distinct areas: the *continental shelf,* the *continental slope,* and the *floor of the ocean.* The continental shelf is a band of gradually sloping sea bottom surrounding all the continents on earth. Sunlight penetrates most of it to a varying degree. Vegetation similar to land vegetation grows here, and the bottom is covered with sand and soil washed from the land. Common species of salt-water fish are found here. Because it is shallow, most of our present knowledge about the ocean has been obtained from the continental shelf areas.

What are the three areas of the ocean bottom?

At one time, the 100-fathom (600 feet) line was generally accepted as the line of separation or demarcation between the continental shelf and slope. At the present time, however, most oceanographers mark the division wherever the relatively gentle slope of the shelf suddenly changes to a very steep one. The world over, the average depth at which this change occurs is at about 72 fathoms, although there are some spots off the Antarctic continent where the shelf ends at between 200 and 300 fathoms.

On the Pacific coast of the United States, the shelf is relatively narrow — not much more than 20 miles wide. On the Atlantic coast, the shelf is usually much wider. Somewhat north of Cape Hatteras, off North Carolina, it is as much as 150 miles wide; yet at the Cape itself and off certain parts of Florida, the plunge begins almost immediately.

Beyond the continental shelf, no matter how deep nor how far from land, the bottom drops off abruptly. If you could descend to the continental slope, and oceanographers are planning to do just this some day, it would be a new and uncomfortable world. There is little light and no plant life; the pressure, cold, and silence increase; the scenery is mud, rocks, and clay; it is inhabited by large and small carnivorous animals, such as those encountered only in nightmares.

What is the continental slope like?

The continental slopes are among the most imposing features of the entire earth; they are the longest and highest

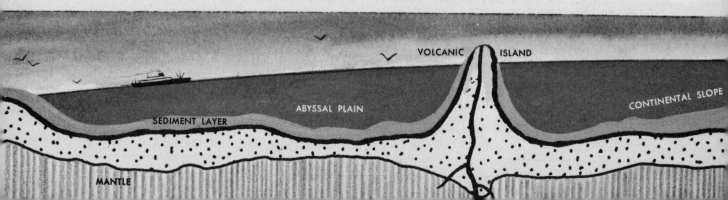

MANTLE · SEDIMENT LAYER · ABYSSAL PLAIN · VOLCANIC ISLAND · CONTINENTAL SLOPE

continuous boundary walls in the world. One of the most spectacular features of the slopes are tremendous submarine canyons with their steep cliffs and winding valleys. These canyons have been found by soundings and, in all probability, are of world-wide occurrence. Geologically speaking, they are relatively young — no more than a million or so years old. But how and why they were formed is a mystery.

There are dozens of such canyons or gorges along the continental slopes. The spectacular Grand Canyon could, in some cases, be dropped into one of these with hardly more than a splash. They are usually found near the mouth of a continental river. For example, the most completely surveyed submarine canyon in the Western North Atlantic is the Hudson Canyon. This extends from the 100-fathom curve, 90 miles southeast of New York harbor to a 2650-fathom plain some 300 miles off shore. This 200-mile long canyon is a chasm 1000 feet deep in places and has several sizable tributaries entering it. The canyon cuts through the continental slope and joins a depression in the continental shelf which marks the entrance of the Hudson River channel off New York harbor. In this instance, the Hudson Canyon system acts as a passageway down which sediment is carried by currents to the deep sea bottom which, at this spot, is an enormous plain of mud.

What is the floor of the deep ocean like?

The ocean floor lies at the foot of the continental slope and is the true bottom of the ocean. This area, often called the *abyss*, holds the mysteries of a strange, unknown world. Actually, the floor of the deep ocean is the last

Our recently acquired knowledge of the characteristics of the ocean floor is based on the three methods we have of studying it:

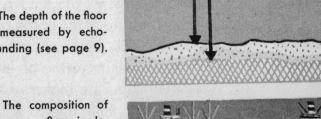

1. The depth of the floor is measured by echo-sounding (see page 9).

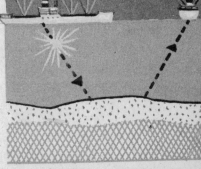

2. The composition of the ocean floor is deduced from seismic surveying. Sound waves from an underwater explosion are triggered by one ship. They are refracted and their traveling time is recorded by a second ship some miles away.

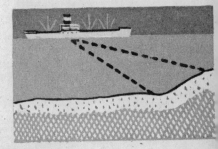

3. The general features of the sea floor are detected with echo-ranging. The difference between 1. and 3. is: in 1., a series of ultrasonic signals are sent straight down to the ocean floor; in 3., they are directed in a narrow, almost horizontal beam and actually sweep out large areas with sound pulses.

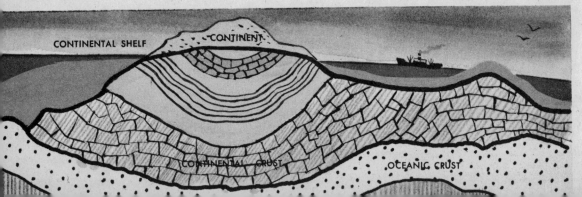

CONTINENTAL SHELF   CONTINENT

CONTINENTAL CRUST   OCEANIC CRUST

Cross-section through the crust of the earth.

large area to be explored on the planet earth. When we do explore the floor of the ocean, what we find there may be as amazing as anything on the planets in outer space.

Most of the work of oceanographers, to the present, has been done from the surface of the ocean. But, the results of their findings give us a good idea of what man may find when he explores the bottom of deep ocean in person. From various sonic soundings, we know that the abyss has a topography or contour much the same as the land mass of the earth. The floor of the deep ocean has mountain ranges, plateaus, canyons, valleys, hills, and plains just as on land. But many mountains are higher, many ranges are longer, many canyons and gorges are deeper than land counterparts. Mount Everest, land's tallest mountain, could be dropped into the great canyons, or *trenches* as they are called, and still be covered by a mile of water.

The average depth of the ocean is between 2¼ and 2½ miles, but there are spots where it is over seven miles deep. The deepest depressions occur not in the center of the ocean's basins, but generally near the continents. The Mindanao Deep, east of the Philippines, is about six and one-half miles deep. The Tuscarora Trench, east of Japan, almost as deep, is one of a series of long narrow trenches that border the outer rim of a chain of islands that includes the Bonins, the Marianas, and the Palaus. The greatest depths of the Atlantic Ocean lie near the West Indies and below Cape Horn.

Explorers have, for a long time, realized **What are ocean islands?** that many of the islands of the ocean are simply the tops of mountains that rise from the floor of the sea. These mountains or *seamounts,* as they are often called, are usually found in groups or ridges just as land mountains are usually found in ranges like the Appalachians in the eastern part of the United States, the Rockies of the west, or the Andes of

Atlantic Seascape.

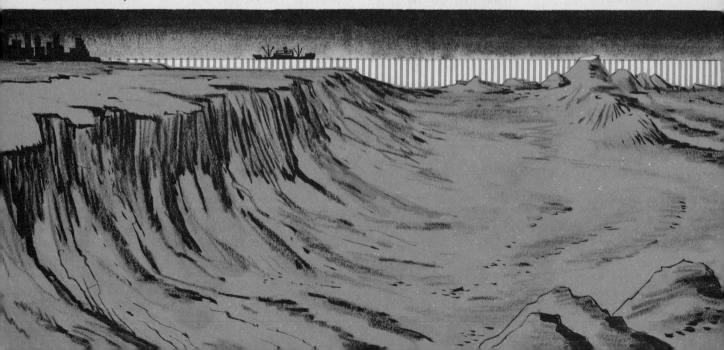

Pacific Seascape.

South America. Most of the islands of the Central Atlantic, for example, are peaks of the Mid-Atlantic Ridge. The Hawaiian Islands, in the central Pacific Ocean, are peaks along the top of a great submarine ridge more than 1,600 miles long. The Marshall Islands in the western Pacific, are coral caps on great volcanoes. Thousands of other mountains rise from the bottom of the Pacific but do not quite reach the surface.

Among the most interesting mountains on earth are the **Where are the largest mountains on earth?** Mid-Pacific Mountains, a submarine range extending from the vicinity of Necker Island of the Hawaiian group to the vicinity of Wake Island. Material obtained by dredging and coring along the tops and upper sides of these mountains has provided clues as to their origin. This material consisted of pebbles, cobbles, and boulders of basalt, many of which appeared to have been rounded by the action of rivers or beach waves, and of limestone containing coral about 100 million years old. Geologists and other scientists concluded that, during the time when dinosaurs still roamed the continents, this undersea range formed a chain of islands.

At that time, the sea eroded the projecting peaks of the chain to flat surfaces. Reef coral larvae drifted to the islands, probably from the east, and lodged on and among the debris. In the warm tropical surface waters, enough of the corals grew and accumulated to form banks. There were not enough of these, however, to conceal the rocks and finer sediments (soil and mud) and thus form the islands or atolls.

Probably, as a result of adjustments of the earth's crust, the great range sank, at first fast enough to kill the reef coral, then more slowly until the present depth was reached.

The Mid-Pacific Mountains may be older, but the Atlantic Ocean has the biggest range of mountains. It winds

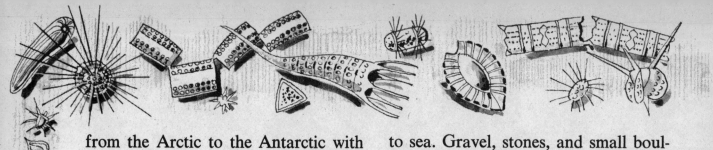

from the Arctic to the Antarctic with peaks averaging 10,000 feet. One undersea giant, Pico, in the Azores, rises 27,000 feet. Known as the Mid-Atlantic Ridge, this chain of submarine peaks and plateaus runs the length of the vast S-shaped trough of the Atlantic. The range, 10,000 miles in length, is about twice as wide as the Andes and several times the width of the Appalachians. The greater part of the Ridge is, of course, submerged. The central backbone rises 5,000 to 10,000 feet above the sea floor, but there is another mile of water above most of its summits. Rock-forming materials, welling up very slowly from below the earth's crust, made the Ridge. In 1970, scientists learned that this continuing process is spreading the ocean floor and pushing North and South America apart from Europe and Africa.

While there are a few spots on the floor of the deep sea where the underlying rock is exposed, the vast majority is cover matter which has settled from the water above. Oceanographers call this matter *sediment* or *ooze*. In addition to the mud and silt of every river on land that empties into the ocean, other materials make up the sediment on the bottom of the sea. Volcanic dust, which may have been blown halfway around the world, eventually finds its way to the ocean, floats for a while on the surface, then sinks. Dust from the desert is blown out

What lies on the bottom of the deep sea?

to sea. Gravel, stones, and small boulders, picked up by glaciers, fall to the bottom when the ice melts. Meteoric debris that enters the earth's atmosphere over the oceans finds its way to the bottom. But, as great as the total of this material may be, it is of minor importance compared to the billions upon billions of tiny shells and skeletons of the very, very small creatures which, for millions of years, have lived near the surface of the sea and then, upon death, have drifted downward to the very bottom.

Near the continents, on the edges of the continental slopes, is just plain mud — blue, green, red, black, or white — washed out to sea by the rivers. Farther out, the fine mud or ooze is composed primarily of the shells of the tiny, one-celled creatures called *globigerina*.

The sea floor over large areas in the temperate zone is covered with these shells. Over the ages, the species have varied somewhat so that it is possible to estimate the age of the deposit by the type of their shells. Although each shell is small, in number they have covered millions of square miles of ocean bottom, sometimes to a depth of thousands of feet.

The discarded shells of other living creatures also cover the bottom. *Radiolarians,* similar in appearance to snowflakes, form broad bands of sediment or ooze in the North Pacific. *Diatoms,* the microscopic plant life of the sea, are so abundant in the sea that their total weight is estimated at more than that

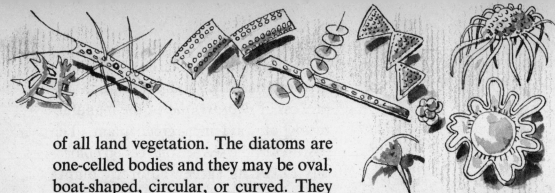

The remains of small animals and plants such as plankton, radiolaria, diatoms, and many other such forms of life that once existed near the sea's surface form much of the sediment on the ocean floor.

of all land vegetation. The diatoms are one-celled bodies and they may be oval, boat-shaped, circular, or curved. They make up large bands of sediment in deep water. When this diatom ooze is raised up from the bottom and allowed to dry out, it becomes what is known as *diatomaceous earth*. This substance is used as insulating material against sound and heat, as a filler in making cement and rubber, as a filter, as a binder in the preparation of dynamite, and because of its abrasive properties, it is employed extensively in scouring powders and even toothpastes. Other uses of diatomaceous earth may be found in the future, as well as uses for some of the other types of ooze and sediment that are so plentiful on the ocean's bottom.

Until a few years ago, no one could **How deep is this sediment?** have answered the question with any assurance. Now, thanks to modern scientific methods such as those described on page 10, we have a fair idea as to how deep the sediment is. In some spots it is very thin and in others it is very deep. In the Atlantic basin of the world ocean, for example, sediment layers of 12,000 feet — ten times taller than the Empire State Building — have been found. No sediment layers thicker than 1,000 feet have been found in either the Pacific Ocean or the Indian Ocean and, in some spots, it has been less than 100 feet.

As the approach to the foothills of the Atlantic Ridge from the American side of the ridge begins, the sediments deepen as though they were mammoth snow drifts — snow drifts 1,000 to 2,000 feet deep against the slope. Farther up the Ridge, where occasionally the terrain flattens out into plateaus, the drifts increase at times to 3,000 feet. The peaks are bare.

Life Within the Ocean

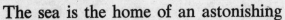

The sea is the home of an astonishing **What type of life exists in the ocean?** variety of living things, from microscopic creatures to giant 100-foot-long, 150-ton blue whales — more than three times as heavy as any dinosaur that ever lived. In the life within the ocean, the oceanographer may find many of the answers to life on earth that existed thousands of years ago, as well as means to improve man's living in the future.

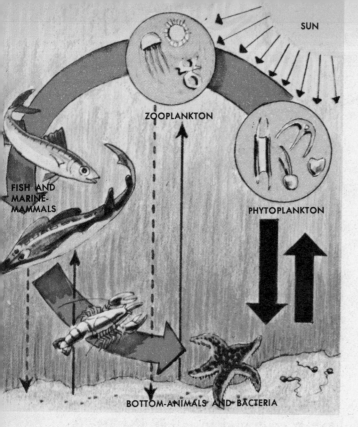

Life and food cycle in the ocean.

In the sea as on the land, the life cycle is supported by sunlight through the process of *photosynthesis,* the manufacturing of food in a green plant. The pastures of the sea are one-celled chlorophyll-bearing (green-colored) plants called *phytoplankton.* They are the food for the *zooplankton,* free-floating or weakly-swimming animals of many shapes and sizes. The zooplankton, in turn, feed the carnivores (flesh-eaters) of the ocean and, of course, the big carnivores eat the little ones. Death and decomposition complete the cycle. The organic material of both plants and animals is subject to bacterial decay which again releases the raw materials — carbon, phosphorus, and nitrogen — needed for the process of photosynthesis. Because organic matter sinks, much of the decomposition and decay occurs in deep water, well below the sunlit areas in which photosynthesis must take place. However, the essential

For this reason, nature's life cycle in the sea, and the way it works, is more important to the oceanographer than the individual plants and animals that live within the ocean.

Life at the edge of the sea.

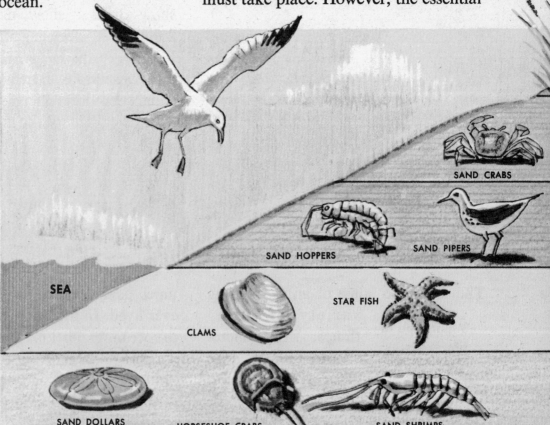

elements are eventually returned to the surface by oceanic currents.

Light sufficient for photosynthesis can penetrate to depths of only about 300 feet in the clearest ocean water. Although phytoplankton can survive only in these shallow areas, animal life has been found in all parts of the ocean, even at the bottom of the deepest part. At these great depths, we do not know how the life cycle is carried on, and may not know until man explores the floor of the ocean in person. We must remember that while a great deal is known about life in the ocean, much still remains a mystery.

The greatest population and variety of marine life is found close to the shore. But at the shoreline itself, the creatures of the sea exist under the most difficult of conditions. As the tide

What kind of life exists at the edge of the sea?

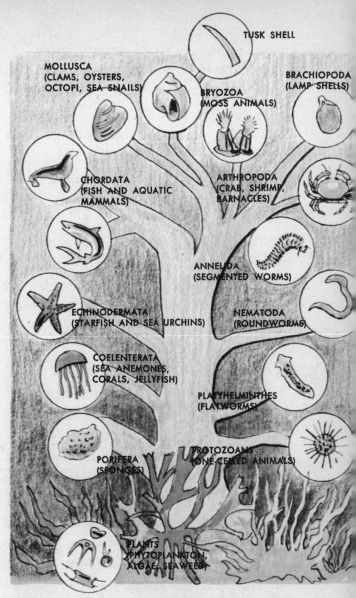

Life in the sea, from which all life evolved, ranges from the most simple, the protozoan, to the most complex forms of fish and sea-mammals.

rises and falls, they are exposed to drying, flooding, baking, and freezing. In addition, they must face the power and danger of waves. Most animals that live at the edge of the sea are streamlined or flattened, so that water rolls easily over them. Some, like the starfish and limpets, have suction-type devices which hold them tight against the rocks. Many, like snails and barnacles, can protect themselves by withdrawing into their shells. Barnacles attach themselves to rocks and pier pilings by using a spe-

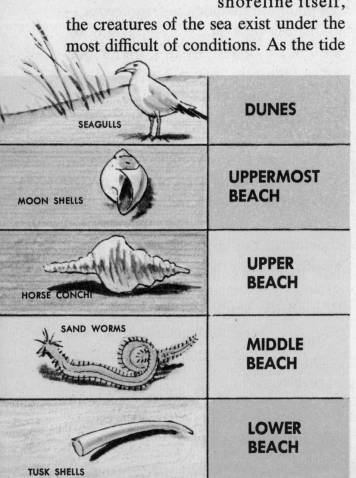

SEAGULLS	**DUNES**
MOON SHELLS	**UPPERMOST BEACH**
HORSE CONCHI	**UPPER BEACH**
SAND WORMS	**MIDDLE BEACH**
TUSK SHELLS	**LOWER BEACH**

cial gland to pour a chemical over them. This firmly anchors them and there they stay the rest of their lives. Rocky hollows also offer shelter to sponges, sea anemones, and sea urchins.

The shoreline animals that live on sandy beaches, such as crabs, sand worms, clams, and cockles, find their protection by burrowing into the sand. While most sea animals will die if they are kept in the air too long, the seashore type can remain in the air from one high tide to the next.

The shallow water beyond the low tide level supports thousands upon thousands of species of animals and plants. As a matter of fact, most of the continental shelf is very well populated since plant life is able to attach itself to the bottom as well as remain within range of sunlight. Plants, in turn, attract many animals. *Algae* are the number one phytoplankton of the sea. They vary in size from microscopic single cells such as diatoms to the many-celled seaweed, which grows in the Pacific to the size of a large tree, 100 to 150 feet in length. In the matter of color, the algae also vary widely. On this basis, four color classes are well known — blue greens, greens, browns, and reds. They all contain chlorophyll and can make their own food. Algae can survive, as long as there is sunlight, in almost any kind of sea environment, as well as along the shoreline. The seashore types anchor themselves to rocks by means of a root-like process called a holdfast.

What type of life exists in the shallow sea?

Except for algae, many one-celled marine bacteria, and some grasslike plants like eel grass, turtle grass, and manatee grass, the sea is relatively barren of plant life. While some marine fungi are present, there are no ferns, mosses, or other lower members of the plant kingdom in the world ocean. No highly evolved members of the plant family like the trees and flowering plants that are found on land exist in the sea. (See page 40.)

The smallest animals representative of zooplankton are the one-celled *protozoans,* of which the jellyfish are among the largest. Other members of this group include corals, anemones, a large number of tiny creatures and larvae or young forms of oysters, snails, and worms that live off of the phytoplankton. The more developed animals of the zooplankton include the *crustaceans* — crabs, shrimps and lobsters, and the *mollusks* — clams, oysters, squids, abalones, mussels, octopi, and scallops. These animals eat the smaller species of zooplankton and graze upon phytoplankton.

The higher forms of zooplankton are in turn eaten by all sorts of larger undersea creatures, from small fishes such as herring, menhaden, sardines, and anchovies, to the largest mammals in the world, the giant toothless sperm whales.

Beyond the shallow continental shelf, animals live a very different sort of life; there is no plant life. In general, oceanic waters cannot be compared with the shallow sea in richness and variety of swimming

What is life like in the open ocean?

DEADMAN'S FINGER SPONGE

Sponges are plant-like animals that grow on the ocean bottom and feed on small water-animals. Before artificial sponges were manufactured, sponge-diving was part of an important industry.

SHEEP'S WOOL SPONGE

GRASS SPONGE

GLOVE SPONGE

life. In the open sea, food is scarce and the animals that live there find their meals at irregular intervals. Many animals in this region come to the surface to feed on zooplankton. Others, however, feed upon smaller fish or dead matter, which drift down from the upper waters. (See page 41.)

There are, however, some "regions of plenty" in truly deep waters. They are the oceanic currents. Marine biologists believe that only migrating or spawning fish such as the sea bass, albacore, cod, and mackerel frequent the currents themselves. But along the edges of these currents live the mighty marlin, the sailfish, speedy tuna, and other big-game fish. Such a location permits them to swim into the fast-moving current and grab a passing migrating fish for dinner.

There are also regions of plenty on the high plateaus, called *banks*, that rise from the ocean's floor. These high areas in the deep ocean have many of the same conditions that exist in the

shallow sea. Most of these spots offer abundant fishing grounds for the commercial fishermen; the three best known are north of Japan, the Newfoundland Banks off Canada, and Georges Bank off Massachusetts. (See page 41.)

The eternal night of the deep ocean is the home of the oddest animals that anyone can imagine. They look nothing like any of the other inhabitants of the sea. While most of them are small, scaleless, and flabby, their shapes vary greatly. Many of these deep-sea dwellers are snakelike, some are pencil-shaped or arrow-shaped with narrow fins running all around their bodies; others are almost as round as

What is life like in the deep ocean?

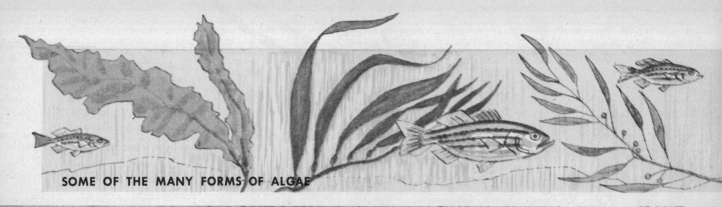

SOME OF THE MANY FORMS OF ALGAE

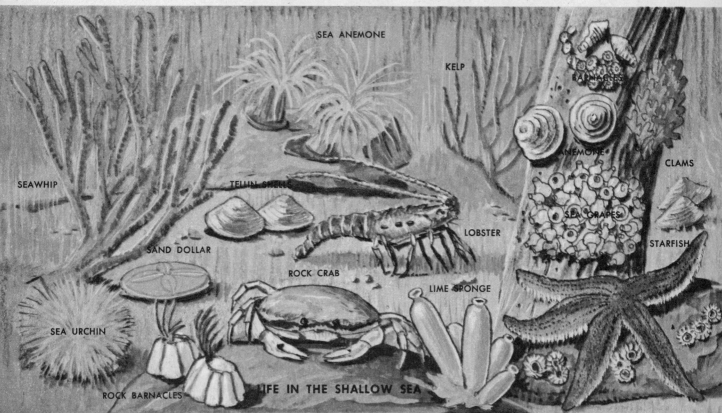

SEA ANEMONE

KELP

BARNACLES

SEAWHIP

CLAMS

TELLIN SHELLS

ANEMONE

LOBSTER

SEA GRAPES

SAND DOLLAR

STARFISH

ROCK CRAB

LIME SPONGE

SEA URCHIN

ROCK BARNACLES

LIFE IN THE SHALLOW SEA

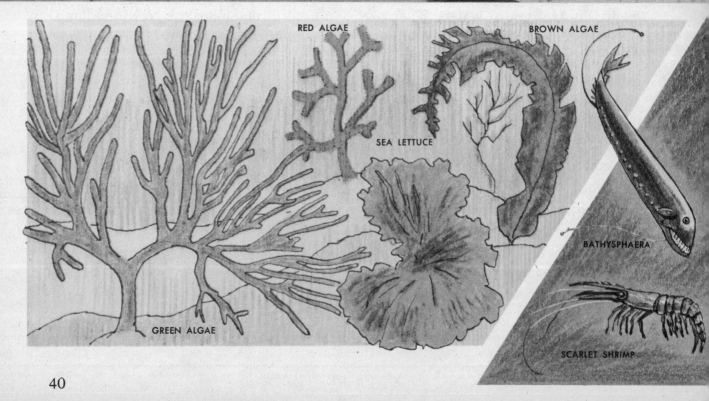

RED ALGAE

BROWN ALGAE

SEA LETTUCE

BATHYSPHAERA

GREEN ALGAE

SCARLET SHRIMP

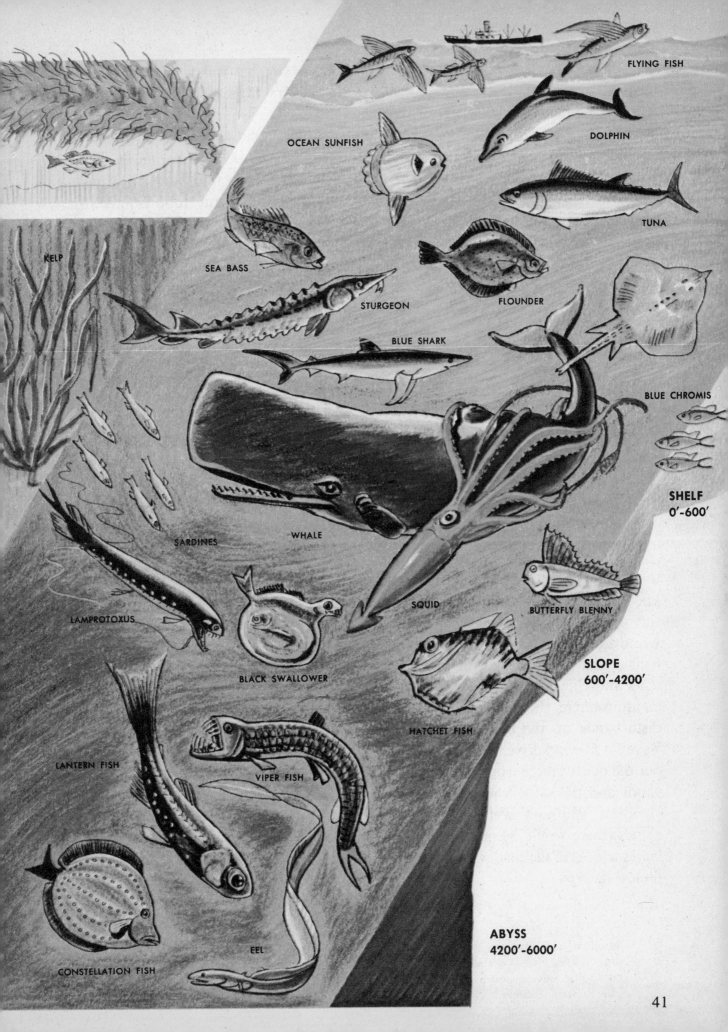

FLYING FISH

DOLPHIN

OCEAN SUNFISH

TUNA

SEA BASS

FLOUNDER

KELP

STURGEON

BLUE SHARK

BLUE CHROMIS

SHELF
0'-600'

SARDINES

WHALE

SQUID

BUTTERFLY BLENNY

LAMPROTOXUS

BLACK SWALLOWER

SLOPE
600'-4200'

HATCHET FISH

LANTERN FISH

VIPER FISH

ABYSS
4200'-6000'

CONSTELLATION FISH

EEL

41

the full moon. Most have developed long, needle-sharp teeth and mouths that are tremendous for the size of their bodies. Also, most of these fish are black in color and many in the deepest waters are blind, having no need for eyes in this pitch-black world of the abyss. Others have eyes which bulge like golf balls, while some have luminescent filaments or spots, which glow in the dark. How this living light is used by these creatures of the perpetual darkness is hard to say, but it is generally believed that it attracts their food, their mates, or both.

Little is known about the feeding habits of the deep-sea animals. Some scientists believe that bacteria provide the most important food source for them, while others think that they feed on each other. Like most other phases of marine biology, we are just beginning to understand the complex pattern of marine life. (See page 41.)

The Air Above the Ocean

While the oceanographer is primarily

Why is the atmosphere above the ocean important?

concerned with the action of the ocean and life under its surface, he must also have knowledge about the atmosphere above the ocean. The atmosphere and the world ocean are partners in the great heat engine which drives the wind systems and the ocean currents. Without an atmosphere, there would be no wind disturbance on the ocean surface, no waves nor wind-driven currents; without the ocean, there would be no water vapor and the skies would be dry and cloudless. Without water vapor and clouds, there would be no rain and the land surfaces of the earth would become lifeless deserts.

The sun, air, and ocean water work

How does the atmospheric heat engine work?

together as interlocking parts in what oceanographers call the *atmospheric heat engine*. The power supply for this engine is the unequal heating of the earth by the sun. As the sun warms the ocean water, most of

Based on knowledge gathered by oceanographers, meteorologists are now able to predict our weather more accurately. At right, a weather man at work charting the track of a storm.

the heat energy is consumed in evaporation or is absorbed by the water; the air above the ocean does not become greatly heated. The land masses on earth, on the other hand, absorb only six-tenths as much heat as the ocean water does, and evaporation is less. Hence, the air over the land tends to receive a greater share of heat than does the air over water. This warm air on land tends to expand and become lighter. Thus, the air over the sea is

The salt from a droplet of sea water that is squirted into the winds can become the "seed" which might release the rain from the clouds.

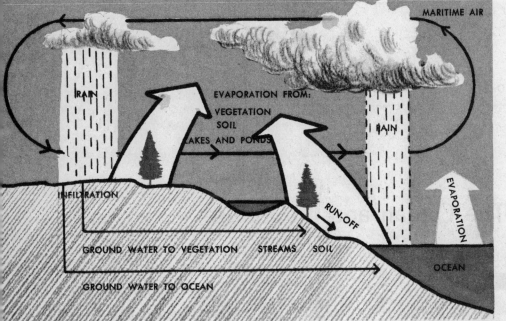

A graphic illustration of the *water cycle* shows how the working of the *atmospheric heat engine* prevents the oceans from drying out. (Based on illustration by U.S. Dept. of Agriculture.)

denser or heavier than the land air. Because it is heavier, its pressure near the earth's surface is greater. This extra pressure starts it flowing landward where it pushes the lighter land air up out of the way. This results in on-shore winds, those that blow from the sea.

As we have already said, the sun's heat evaporates water from the ocean and water vapor gathers in the form of clouds. The wind may blow these clouds over land. When the water vapor of the clouds is cooled, perhaps many thou-

sands of miles from their ocean birthplace, the moisture is dropped in the form of rain or snow. Thus, the atmospheric heat engine could be called *nature's rain* or *weather maker*.

The ocean does not dry up because when the rain or snow falls, it either drops back into the ocean or sinks into the ground, feeds the streams and rivers, and eventually returns to the ocean. This over-all working of the atmospheric heat engine is called the *water cycle*. As explained earlier, winds and

43

the unequal heating of the earth by the sun are also responsible for waves and oceanic currents.

If oceanographers can solve all mysteries of the atmospheric heat engine, they will know more about the waves and oceanic currents. Working with meteorologists, they may be able to control weather and may perfect the process of artifical rainmaking. If we know fully how the atmospheric engine converts and utilizes its ocean water supply, it would be possible to change parched deserts into useful land.

Drilling operation for oil from deposits under the ocean floor.

The Ocean and the Future

New fishing methods: Fish, attracted by underwater lights, are sucked aboard by pumps.

What food do we get from the sea? The prime purpose of the oceanographer's work is to obtain knowledge about the world ocean so that it can be used for the benefit of man. For example, he has learned through studies that the ocean is a vast storehouse of foodstuffs. But, at the present time, the only food that is taken in large quantities is fish. In countries such as Japan, fish form the most important part of the protein diet. But, of the whole world's protein available for human consumption, fish·account for only a little over one per cent. With growing world populations to feed, however, it is certain that the world's

Salt can be obtained from sea water that has been permitted to evaporate under the sun's rays.

Settling tanks used in the process of extracting magnesium from sea water.

Valuable iodine can be derived from seaweed. However, the machinery is complicated and the yield small compared to the cost.

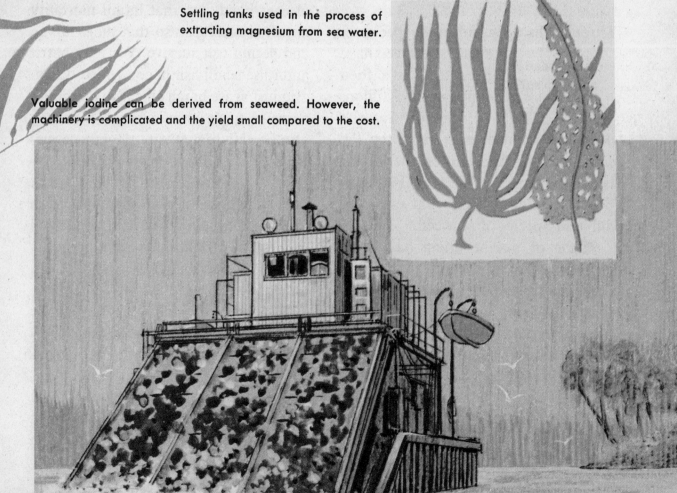

fisheries will have to increase their harvest, and we are sure that the sea can give this increase if we can learn better ways to gather and care for its resources.

Although the fishing boats use modern navigation, echo-sounders, and aircraft to spot their catches, they employ methods, such as lines, nets, and trawls, which have not changed for hundreds of years. However, as the needs of the world for food increase, new and different ways of fishing will be used. Today in the Caspian Sea, for example, fish are attracted by underwater lights and sucked aboard the fishing vessels by pumps. There will be efficient new methods, too, of finding the fish, thanks to many studies undertaken by marine biologists and oceanographers.

Through the ages, the larger species of algae or seaweed have been used as a food supplement. Millions of people in the densely populated areas along the Pacific Coast of Asia and on the Pacific Islands — Japanese, Chinese, Filipinos, Burmese, Indonesians — eat over 100 different species of seaweed.

Is seaweed good to eat?

Algae of marine origin have been used for centuries as a fertilizer for farm crops and as a food for cattle. Several factories in this country process algae for cattle-feed. Seaweeds, especially the giant kelp plants that grow in the Pacific Ocean, are excellent sources of iodine. To process the plant, the kelp is dried and burned, and the iodine is separated from the ashes. Seaweeds are also processed into a substance called *algin* which is used in cosmetics, textiles, ink, paper, paints, and drugs as well as in chocolate milk, ice cream, cheeses, jellies, and jams.

At one time, the seaweeds were harvested by pulling it from the rocks by hand or cutting it by scythes on long poles. Today ocean-going harvester ships are powered through beds of giant kelp and can reap 25 tons in an hour. After it is gathered, it is dried out or dehydrated before it is processed.

As time goes on, the counterpart of agriculture in the oceans, *aquaculture*, will catch up with the latest agricultural methods on land. We will make sure that a great percentage of eggs hatch and that infant mortality in fish is decreased so that more larvae and young fish survive. We may hatch and raise small fish in controlled oceanaria just as we hatch chicks in a brooder or raise trout in hatcheries. We may also be able to cultivate the most abundant known source of life in the sea — plankton. Many scientists believe that both phytoplankton and zooplankton can some day be raised and controlled to feed the world's skyrocketing population. Whether or not this is true, only time can tell.

What is aquaculture?

To obtain the full potential of the sea as a food source for mankind, it will be necessary to adapt to the oceans such routine farming practices as plowing and fencing. Plowing the ocean will involve speeding up the rate at which the nutrient minerals (the fertilizer) on the bottom are brought to the surface. Atomic reactors to heat the bottom water and make it rise have been suggested. Fences of air bubbles or sound waves might keep the oceanic livestock from wandering; air-bubble fences are now being tried to keep sharks away from beaches in tropical areas. New methods of harvesting the underwater crops will also have to be worked out. While marine biologists and oceanographers are not usually involved in solving problems of this sort, they work on the vital background information on which the answers may be based.

Making fresh water by removing salt

Can fresh water be obtained from the sea?

from sea water is already being done on a large scale in many places, but it is still an expensive process. But, with our ever-increasing demand for fresh water, scientists are working on ways to accomplish it cheaply. One method is to distill the water by boiling it off with the heat of nuclear fuels or the sun's heat and leave the salt behind. An electrical method whereby a current causes positive salt ions to flow in one direction and negative ions in the other, thus separating the salt, is another possibility. Also, there are thin membranes which let pure water through while blocking the flow of salts. Another method simply freezes sea water. The freezing process extracts salt from the water. After the salt has been separated from the ice, the ice is melted, giving fresh water. One of the best methods for obtaining fresh water, called multi-*stage flash distillation,* evaporates sea water rapidly several times, each time in a higher vacuum and at a lower temperature.

The wealth of the sea goes beyond mere

How will mining in the sea be done?

plants, animals, and water. It includes deposits of minerals. Obtaining salt from the sea by evaporation is an ancient industry, and for thousands of years man has taken it for his use by allowing the sun to evaporate the water from shallow salterns. Nowadays, not only sodium salts but potassium and magnesium salts are separated from sea water. Bromine gas, used in the manufacture of ethyl or "anti-knock" gasoline, is a valuable byproduct of both salt works and magnesium production. But the whole question of whether or not we extract any of the other minerals that are present in ocean water depends on whether it competes favorably with obtaining the same substance from somewhere else. It is possible that the development of atomic energy power plants may make mining of the seas much more common and extensive than at present.

Under the more shallow water of the continental shelves, we are now tapping valuable sources of petroleum and will turn to the sea more and more for oil. Petroleum, the stored sunshine of ancient marine animal fossils, lies not only under our land where the sea once was but also four hundred billion barrels of it, about a third of all remaining on earth, wait in reserve under the sea.

How oceanographers suggest mineral deposits be drawn from the ocean floor onto ore barges.

There are also some minerals such as cobalt, iron, copper, nickel, and manganese which lie exposed in plentiful quantities over vast areas of the deep sea. How they formed there over millions of years is not completely understood. But to mine them at depths of two thousand fathoms, some type of huge vacuum cleaner will have to suck them up into the holds of surface ships or submarine robot-operated, caterpillar-tracked earth movers will have to scrape the valuable deposits or nodules into submarine mine hoists.

Is the ocean becoming polluted? At the beginning of the 1970's, it became clear that human beings are polluting the oceans. Oil tankers and offshore oil wells spill great quantities of life-destroying oil into the seas. Coastal cities and thousands of ships dump garbage and sewage into the oceans. If something is not done to stop this pollution, the oceans will become vast sewers.

Our exploration of the last frontier on earth — the ocean — has really just begun. There is so much yet to be learned, and so much to still be accomplished. To learn all the secrets of the mysterious sea, we are depending on oceanographers — the scientists of the world ocean.

Acknowledgements: The author wishes to thank the following for their technical help and use of their illustrations: Woods Hole Oceanographic Institution; the National Academy of Sciences; the United States Navy; the United States Coast Guard; and Dr. Athelstan Spilhaus of the University of Minnesota.